© Assouline, 1999
26-28, rue Danielle Casanova, Paris 75002 France
Tel: + 33 1 42 60 33 84   Fax: + 33 1 42 60 33 85
Internet: http://www.imaginet.fr/assouline

© Adagp, Paris, 1999
for works by its artists.

Copy-editing: Siôn Rees Williams

ISBN: 2 84323 149 3

Colour separation: Gravor S.A. (Switzerland)
Printed and bound by Grafiche Milani (Italy)

CHRISTIE'S

NICHOLAS POWELL

ASSOULINE

On November 19, 1998, the presentation of Van Gogh's tormented and deeply moving *Portrait de l'artiste sans barbe* [*Portrait of the artist without a beard*] caused an expectant hush to fall in Christie's crowded saleroom in New York. Painted in 1889 in the asylum of Saint-Rémy, a gift for the 70th birthday of the artist's mother, the work depicts a clean-shaven Van Gogh wearing a grey shirt against a light green background. One of the very last Van Gogh self-portraits in private hands, the canvas was sold for \$71,502,500 (£42,815,868) by Christopher Burge, chairman of Christie's North and South America, to become the world's third most expensive painting ever sold at auction.

Acquired in 1998 by the French businessman François Pinault (who, as a well-respected art lover and collector has also been a client of the firm for the past twenty-five years), Christie's employs 1,800 people in 116 offices in 42 countries and organizes some 800 auctions every year. During the two and a half centuries since its creation, Christie's, which in 1997, with sales totalling $2 billion (£1.2 billion), beat its old rival Sotheby's to become the largest auction company in the world, has estabished an impressive number of record prices. Van Gogh's *Portrait of Dr. Gachet*, sold for $82.5 million (£49.1 million) in New York in May 1990, remains the most expensive work of art sold at auction in the world. Pontormo's *Portrait of Duke Cosimo I de'Medici*, meanwhile, became the highest priced Old Master painting when it was sold for $35.2 million (£22,3 million) in May 1989. In July 1990, Christie's auctioned the lavish Badminton Cabinet for £8.58 million in London, while Microsoft boss Bill Gates paid $30.8 million for Leonardo da Vinci's *Codex Hammer* manuscript at a Christie's sale in New York in 1994.

C hristie's was founded during the second half of the eighteenth century in London, a city in which writers, artists and well-heeled art collectors mixed freely: "When a man is tired of London, he is tired of life; for there is in London all that life can afford", Dr Samuel Johnson said in 1777. Britain was prosperous. Artistic and literary activity was encouraged by a growing international trade and the wealth of a newly-founded Empire, while enthusiasm for collecting art, encouraged by the tradition of the Grand Tour embarked on by Britain's young aristocrats, was reaching new heights. Significantly, gambling was all the rage among the rich and debts incurred at the card table were the only ones that a gentleman was honour-bound to settle straight away; London, in a word, was the ideal place for auctioneering to develop. The excitement of gambling, the fear of losing a coveted object, the hope that is born with each bid; who, among today's auction-goers, can claim in conscience that he or she has never gone beyond the financial limits they had sensibly set themselves before the sale?

around 1760, a young Scotsman, James Christie, who had served in the Royal Navy, began working with a certain Mr Annesley, an auctionner in the highly fashionable district of Covent Garden. Not long afterwards he set up his own business before moving to an even more fashionable address – 125 Pall Mall in the heart of St. James's, where the British nobility had their town houses. Christie's neighbour was the painter Thomas Gainsborough, with whom he quickly became firm friends and who later painted his portrait. At the start of his career James Christie, like all his colleagues, sold everything: his first catalogue of 5 December 1766 lists, among other items, two chamber pots, *Moonlight*, a painting by the seventeenth-century Dutch artist Jacob Gerrittsz Cuyp, sold for £3 11s., a pair of sheets, two pillowcases and four irons. On another occasion, James Christie sold a coffin, the owner of which had made "a most remarkable recovery from a malady usually regarded by the medical confraternity as fatal."

Unlike his competitors, James Christie quickly specialized in the sale of art. His first sale of paintings, which included Italian, French and Flemish works, attributed to Andrea del Sarto,

Tintoretto, Poussin, Rembrandt and Titian, many of them doubtless copies, as was the fashion at the time, was organised on 20 and 21 March 1767. During a career embracing some 1,200 sales, James Christie turned what had been a lowly administrative job into an art in its own right: wearing a grey wig, spectacles perched on his forehead, he conducted sales, gavel in hand, from behind a tall rostrum. Famed for his eloquence and humour, nicknamed "the king of epithets", he knew how to tease the hesitant bidder to the delight of saleroom crowds. His success was rapid. Members of the aristocracy and even the Royal Family began to consign works to him, while the best informed collectors – frequently the same individuals –, attended his sales. The intellectual élite of the day, from the painter Sir Joshua Reynolds to the playwright and politician Richard Sheridan, the writer Horace Walpole and the actor David Garrick all became friends of James Christie. Evening exhibitions in his saleroom, with their carefully selected visitors, resembled a highly fashionable *salon*, and became major attractions on every smart Londoner's social agenda.

business boomed. So, too, did the stories. In 1784, James Christie sold books, manuscripts, furniture and jewellery belonging to the famed French transvestite spy Charles de Beaumont, chevalier d'Eon. Beaumont, who upon his return to France in 1777 after carrying out a secret assignment for Louis XV at the court of Catherine the Great had been ordered never to remove his female clothes, was tactfully described in the sales catalogue as "a lady of fashion and an officer of Dragoons." The French Revolution of 1789, which effectively displaced the international art market from Paris to London, made James Christie a rich man. Wave upon wave of émigré aristocrats arrived in London bringing with them furniture, paintings and jewels which were quickly auctioned off to meet the financial burden of living in exile. While British dealers visited Versailles to buy up the furniture of the most sumptuous of French royal residences, James Christie's London catalogues began announcing the sale of collections belonging to "Foreign gentlemen of Distinction" and other various "French noblemen."

a fter the execution of Marie-Antoinette in 1793, James Christie auctioned the Queen's paintings from the Château de Saint Cloud, near Paris. Meanwhile, Louis XV's former mistress Madame du Barry, frightened by the death of her lover and protector the Duc de Brissac, crossed the Channel no fewer than four times during the Revolution in the hope of recovering her fabulous collection of jewellery, which had surfaced in London after being stolen from her château in Louveciennes. Betrayed by her servant Zamor, she was guillotined in 1793. Two years later, James Christie sold the extensive collection of fine quality diamonds and pearls of "Madame la Comtesse Dubarry, deceased", listed in a two-page catalogue, for the sum of £13,412 9s 3d – the equivalent of some $2.7 million (£1.7 million) in today's currency. For all the glamour of such sales and the extremely large sums of money involved, James Christie remained a level-headed businessman. Only a few weeks before the Madame du Barry sale, and doubtless with the same panache, he auctioned "About 72 loads of excellent meadow hay" from a farm only a few miles away from St James's.

On James Christie's death in 1803, his son, also James, took over the firm, which he moved, in 1823, into its present premises on King Street, close to Pall Mall. During the nineteenth century, Christie's began a new speciality, the sale of the contents of stately homes, or "house sales". A common enough event nowadays, these sales at first alarmed the upper classes. In 1848, the contents of the Duke of Buckingham's vast and splendid home Stowe House, built in the international baroque style, lasted for thirty-seven days and raised £77,562 4s 6d. The spectacle of a great British aristocratic family reduced to selling off its possessions proved all the more upsetting for members of the landed gentry as thousands of people of uncomfortably modest extraction went to the pre-sale showings to gape. Special trains were even arranged. Carriages and carts, laden down with every member of the family and crammed with food, were rented for a good day out at Stowe. To make matters worse, were that possible, sightseers picnicked in the gardens. "An ancient family ruined, their palace marked for destruction, and its contents scattered to the four winds of Heaven", bemoaned *The Times*, which, in the same tragic vein, devoted a long article to the sale. Ironically enough, the owners of Stowe were later able to buy back and re-establish most of the important objects sold in 1848. Until, that is, fresh financial worries in 1922 obliged them to sell both the house and contents for good.

the most important house sale of the century was Hamilton Palace in Scotland in 1882, organized not on account of financial embarrassment but because the 10th Duke of Hamilton could no longer abide the numerous coal mines and factories which were springing up around his home. Worthy of a museum, the colossal collection of paintings, objets d'art and furniture housed in Hamilton Palace – not itself of any great architectural note –, included more than a hundred outstanding British, Dutch, Flemish and Spanish canvases; high quality Chinese, French, Italian and Japanese porcelain; a superb Louis XIV commode and cabinet by Boulle; furniture by Gouthière and Riesener which had belonged to Marie-Antoinette; not to mention the ill-fated Madame du Barry's *secrétaire*, Limoges enamels, vases in Egyptian porphyry and ancient coins; 2,213 lots all in all, sold over a period of seventeen days for a colossal total of £397,562 0s. 6d.

While significant amounts of Britain's national heritage began to pass through King Street, successive political crises in France also gave rise to some spectacular sales. Louis-Philippe's Spanish Gallery in the Louvre, acquired with his personal wealth, was closed in the wake of the revolution of 1848. The paintings remained there until October 1850, when they were dispatched, without their frames and very poorly packed, to the dead king's family who had taken refuge in England. Christie's auction of the 528 paintings – one of the largest, if not the largest collection of Spanish Old Masters ever assembled –, lasted six days in May 1853. The sale was evidently the major event of the year. Velázquez attracted by far the highest bids; his *Adoration of the Shepherds* was sold to the National Gallery for over £2,000, a huge sum, only to be re-attributed, much later, as "School of Naples." Works by Murillo, on the other hand, fetched bids of only a few hundred pounds, whilst some Riberas and Zurbarans went for as little as twenty or thirty pounds. Goya was the least appreciated of all. His magnificent *Portrait of the*

Duchess of Alba went under the hammer for a mere six pounds, while *The Old Women*, a masterpiece today in the Palais des Beaux-Arts in Lille, France, was dispatched for a meagre £4 15s.

Collectors at the time were in the habit of purchasing paintings not in galleries but in King Street and Christie's was very sensitive to the prevailing tastes of the day. When Turner briefly went out of fashion, the artist was obliged to bid for his own paintings in order to preserve their market value. Despite such dips in the prices of individual artists, Christie's nevertheless continued to exert an attraction for art enthusiasts. *The Times* wrote in 1875: "Of all the art exhibitions in London, the most agreeable is that which is always open throughout the spring and summer months in King Street, St James's. With a constantly changing programme, and its prices varying from a guinea to ten thousand, it is ... (a) ... complete mirror of the wealth and taste and fashion of the period."

Some artistic reputations never waned. The works of the portraitist and landscape artist Sir Edwin Landseer, for example, much appreciated by Queen Victoria and Prince Albert, were particularly sought after. So too, from the 1860s, were those of the Pre-Raphaelite painters such as Edward Burne-Jones and John Everett Millais, whose idealised and courtly world proved particularly pleasing to the rising class of industrialists. Less trained in the appreciation of art than the landed aristocracy, the nouveaux riches nevertheless intended to consolidate their place in society by surrounding themselves with things of beauty.

During the second half of the nineteenth century an ever widening gap opened up between official and high priced salon artists on the one hand and those, predominantly French painters, who were exploring completely fresh artistic avenues on the other. Christie's certainly had no time for Impressionism, the market value of which was then extremely low. Old Masters still ruled the auction room: in 1876, Gainsborough's *Portrait of the Duchess of Devonshire*, painted a century earlier, became the first work ever to be sold at auction for more than £10,000. Seven years later, one of the most expensive paintings sold at Christie's was *The Roses of Heliogabalus*, depicting a banquet at which the mad Roman Emperor suffocates his guests under a deluge of rose petals, by the greatly renowned Sir Lawrence Alma-Tadema. His work later slumped into a commercial purgatory from which it only began to emerge at the end of the twentieth century: in 1993, the same canvas was sold for over £1.6 million, a record for the artist.

In 1900, a collection of Napoleon Bonaparte memorabilia was sold at Christie's for £294. It included a bronze death mask, a lock of hair, a piece of the Emperor's coffin and a "sheet of paper found in his carriage after the battle of Waterloo." Five years later, the same collection, minus a few miniatures and the mysterious piece of paper, was again sold for only £136.

t he art market came to a halt for the First World War, during which Christie's organized sales for the benefit of the Red Cross. Afterwards, King Street continued to attract the belongings of what remained of international royalty. The jewels of Queen Amelia of Portugal were sold there. Also, in 1924, and for a meagre £1,000 was a small collection of lace, furs and clothes belonging to Napoleon III's widow Eugenie, who had died in Paris four years previously, aged 94. In 1927, Christie's auctioned a magnificent selection of mostly eighteenth-century Russian crown jewels, including a 41.37 carat diamond mounted in a brooch, for £11,800.

During the 1930s, Christie's held an average of five sales a week and auctioned around 20,000 objects per year. Seriously damaged during an air raid in 1941, the King Street premises eventually reopened in 1953. Selling for the most part to dealers, Christie's, by now a well-established institution, began to content itself with a steady flow of business like a sort of gentleman's club of the art market. But its turnover was also trailing seriously behind that of its great rival Sotheby's, an even older establishment which had begun specializing in the sale of art much later than Christie's. At the same time, London began to lose its place as undisputed capital of the world's art market. It was high time to react, and an upsurge was not long in coming.

Christie's began to expand towards the end of the 1960s with the firm, just as in the good old days of James Christie, selling everything from works of art to dresses, uniforms and antique toys. With encouraging results, Christie's began to export its expertise. An office had already been opened in Rome in 1958 to attract business. In 1968 the first saleroom outside Britain was opened in Geneva. The same year, Christie's opened their Paris headquarters in the former studio of Max Ernst on rue de Lille. Also in 1970, and to the surprise of most specialists, Velázquez' *Portrait of Juan de Pareja* sold for £2,310,000, becoming the first work of art to sell for more than one million pounds at auction. Five years later, Christie's opened offices in Amsterdam and became a public company quoted on the London Stock Exchange. It was vital not only to sell, but also to attract potential sellers in order to have objects consigned. Representatives were appointed in Melbourne, Montreal, Salzburg, Sydney and Tokyo. In 1975, Christie's opened South Kensington, its second London saleroom.

Real expansion, however, was due to America. The first sale in the US – Impressionist paintings which sold for $834,160 –, took place deep in the heart of Texas, in Houston. The first New York sales, which produced $5 million during the first financial year, followed quickly upon the inauguration in 1977 of Christie's offices on Park Avenue, followed in 1979 by that of a second saleroom: Christie's East.

t hroughout the world, the art market was picking up considerable momentum. The strong but steady expansion of the 1970s (in 1973 alone sales increased by 70 percent in comparison with the previous year) was followed by the arrival of private investment and speculation. For the first time since the end of the eighteenth century, private collectors began to attend sales. Prices skyrocketed. Sales for 1990 reached a total of $2 billion – ten times the figure for 1980.

The first years of the 1980s were characterised by worldwide economic difficulties which, as a luxury sector hypersensitive to such trends, adversely affected the art market. Then between 1982 and 1983, sales increased by a surprising 33 percent. With auctions as outstanding as those of the 78 Italian and Dutch Old Master drawings from the Duke of Devonshire's collection at Chatsworth which sold for £20 million, the period 1983-1984, with growth of 53 percent was deemed "the most memorable season in the firm's long history."

During this period of prosperity, jewellery, which today represents 20 percent of Christie's total sales, acquired a new importance.

Organized in New York on 11 April 1984 in the presence of a black-tie public, the sale of the jewellery belonging to the socialite Florence Gould was as much a social as a commercial event. The auction raised $7.4 million and proved to be the biggest ever sale of its kind. Three years later, also in New York, a red diamond of only 0.95 carats – barely the size of a cherry stone –, was sold for the huge sum of $880,000, effectively launching the fashion for coloured diamonds. Another memorable sale was that of the jewellery of Princess Salimah following her divorce from the Aga Khan. Christie's organized the auction during a long-running legal battle between the couple. The sale finally took place in Geneva on 13 November 1995, just forty-eight hours after being authorised by a local court.

growing speculation in the art market, meanwhile, meant that items which had been virtually unsaleable a few years previously began to be sold with ease. Ever higher record prices were reached, only to be rapidly broken, especially in Impressionist and Modern paintings. In 1987 in London, Van Gogh's *Sunflowers* was sold for an astounding £24.75 million. The following year, also in London, a Picasso gouache, *Acrobate et jeune Arlequin* (1905) went under the hammer for nearly £21 million. The year 1988 saw records established for works by Pierre Bonnard, André Derain, Max Ernst, Pablo Gargallo, Wassily Kandinsky, Paul Klee, Egon Schiele, Nicolas de Staël and Andy Warhol, among others. Unprecedented prices were also paid for items as varied and outstanding in their field as the Fabergé *Pine Cone* egg (1899–1900), sold for 5,280,000 Swiss francs on 10 April 1989 and a tenth-century miniature Koran, which fetched

£176,000 the following day in London. It is well known that Van Gogh never sold a painting during his lifetime, but in 1990 in New York, his *Portrait of Dr. Gachet* attracted a final bid of $82.5 million, the equivalent, in other words, of all Christie's sales in the year 1975. In 1990, Christie's turnover increased by 70 percent. Ignoring the important part played by financial speculation, Lord Carrington, then Chairman of Christie's International, attributed that success to "confidence in our standard of service and integrity", concluding: "What will happen during the next ten years is impossible to predict."

the art market hit a major slump which proved particularly severe for the prices of Impressionist and modern paintings. In its wake, during the early 1990s, Christie's was forced to realign its sales in favour of other collecting specialities. The market changed: in both London and New York, Old Master paintings began to dominate sales and in 1991 the world record auction price was the £7,480,000 paid in Christie's London for *Venus and Adonis* by Titian and his workshop. Record prices were also set in 1991 and 1992 for works by Georges de La Tour and Canaletto. Eight Rubens were auctioned in King Street during the first seven months of 1993. Even Victorian paintings, long despised, made a comeback. Customers bought less but more wisely, demanding quality and provenance first and foremost. The year 1993 was marked by the sale in Monaco of the collection of couturier Hubert de Givenchy, who four years later became President of Christie's France. Comprising 95 outstanding pieces of principally French eighteenth-century furniture and objets d'art, including the famous and lavish Hanover Chandelier, the auction required 30 extra telephone lines to take outside bids and raised 155 million French francs.

Expansion abroad continued. In 1994, by opening an office in Shanghai, Christie's became the first auction company to penetrate the Chinese market. The same year, the sales of furniture and works of art from Houghton Hall in Britain raised a record £21.3 million. As the result of seven discreet years of negotiations, Christie's New York sold Barbra Streisand's collection of Art Nouveau and Art Deco objects. In 1995, in a series of single-owner, celebrity sales, the jewellery of Princess Salimah Aga Khan and the collections of Frank Sinatra and Rudolph Nureyev went under the hammer.

In 1996, for the first time since 1882, a painting by a living artist became the most expensive work of art sold at auction when Willem de Kooning's *Woman* (1949) fetched $15,622,000 (£9.25 million) in New York. While contemporary art began to make a hesitant comeback, Impressionist and Modern paintings again dominated the market. Sold in New York on 10 November 1997 for over $207 million (£122.5 million), the 58 Modern and Contemporary paintings of the Victor and Sally Ganz collection became the most expensive private collection ever sold at auction, helping to make Christie's the world's biggest fine art auction company that year, with sales totalling $2 billion (£1.2 billion).

the anticipated abolition of the four century-old monopoly enjoyed by French auctioneers opens a new chapter in the history of Christie's, which will soon be able to organize sales in France for the first time. The firm is now consolidating its North American operation and moving into France. It is taking

53,800 square feet (5,000 m²) of new premises, including two large salerooms, on avenue Matignon, just off the Champs-Elysées in Paris. In the spring of 1999, Christie's is also doubling the size of its former New York headquarters by inaugurating some 310,000 square feet (29,000 m²) of new offices and three salerooms in the Rockefeller Center, in the heart of Manhattan, next door to the major hotels, restaurants and theatres of New York. Patriotic as he was, that eloquent Scotsman James Christie would surely have approved. The medallion portrait of the *King of Epithets* will be as familiar to art collectors of the twenty-first century as it was to the eighteenth century aristocrats who flocked into Christie's original saleroom in search of the rare and the beautiful.

ELOQUENCE

OR THE KING of EPITHETS

*Let me entreat—Ladies—Gentlemen—permit me
to put this inestimable piece of elegance under your protec-
tion,—only observe,———The inexhaustable Munificence
of your superlitively candid Generosity must HARMONIZE
with the refulgent Brilliancy of this little Jewel! —:—.;*

Pub.ᵈ Jan.ʸ 1.ᵗ 1782 by H.Humphrey Nᵒ 18 New Bond Street

A

CATALOGUE

OF

A most Capital and superb Assemblage of Valuable

JEWELS,

Of most singular Excellence, Beauty, and Perfection,

LATE THE PROPERTY OF

Madame La COMTESSE DUBARRY,

DECEASED.

WHICH (BY ORDER OF THE ADMINISTRATOR)

Will be peremtorily Sold by Auction

By Mr. CHRISTIE,

At his Great Room in Pall Mall,

On THURSDAY, FEBRUARY the 19th, 1795,

Commencing precisely at Half past Twelve o'Clock.

To be Viewed Two Days preceding the Sale; when Catalogues may be had at the
Rainbow Coffee House, Cornhill; and in Pall Mall.

CHRISTIE'S 1766 =

Chinese and Japanese art

+

Sculptu

+

Wine

+

Drawings

+

Books and manuscripts

+

Jewellery

+

Ceramics and glass

+

Textiles

+

Coins

+

Musical
instruments

20th
century art

Textiles
and fans

Furniture

Silver
and objects

Islamic
art

Old master
pictures

Impressionist and
19th century art

CHRISTIE'S
LONDON

£	22500000
$	36292500
SF	54675000
FF	228150000
YN	540000

CHRISTIE'S
LONDON

$$\int \frac{dv}{\sqrt{(r-r')(\ )(\ )(\ )}} = \frac{2\pi}{\sqrt{-\frac{c}{4}}}\left[1 + \frac{1}{4}\frac{\frac{b}{4}}{-\frac{c}{4}} \cdot - \frac{d}{c}\right]$$

$$= \frac{2\pi}{\sqrt{-\frac{c}{4}}}\left[1 + \frac{1}{4}\frac{bd}{c^2}\right]$$

$$\int \frac{dr\left(1 + \alpha\frac{1}{r} + \beta\frac{1}{r^2}\right)}{\sqrt{(r-r_1)(r_2-r)(r-r')(r-v'')}} = I$$

$$\int \frac{dv}{r\sqrt{(r-r_1)(r_2-v)}}\left|\left(1-\frac{r'}{r}\right)^{-\frac{1}{2}}\left(1-\frac{r''}{r}\right)^{-\frac{1}{2}}\left(1+\alpha\frac{1}{r}+\beta\frac{1}{r^2}\right)\right.$$

Faktor auf ∞ Kl. erster Ordnung berechnet

$$\left[1 + \frac{1}{2}(r'+r'')\cdot\frac{1}{r}\right]\left(1+\alpha\frac{1}{r}\right)$$

$$1 + \underbrace{\left(\alpha + \frac{r'+r''}{2}\right)}_{\alpha'}\frac{1}{r}$$

$$I = \int \frac{dr\left(1 + \alpha'\frac{1}{r}\right)}{\sqrt{r(r-r_1)(r_2-r)(r-v')(r-v'')}} = \int \frac{dv\left(1+\alpha'\frac{1}{r}\right)}{r\sqrt{(r-r_1)(r_2-v)}}$$

$$\boxed{\begin{array}{l} I = \int \dfrac{1 + \alpha\frac{1}{2}}{\sqrt{-z^2+az^2+bz+cz+d}}dz \\[2mm] a = z_1 + z_2 + z' + z'' \\ b = z_1 z_2 + (z_1 + z_2)(z'+z'') \\ c = z_1 z_2 (z'+z'') \\ d = 0 \end{array}}$$

$$= \frac{2\pi}{\sqrt{r_1 r_2}}\left[1 + \frac{1}{2}\left(\frac{1}{r_1} + \frac{1}{r_2}\right)\left(\alpha + \frac{r'+r''}{2}\right)\right]$$

$$c_0\, B \int \frac{dr\left(1 - A\frac{1}{r}\right)}{\sqrt{(\mathcal{E}^2-c_0^2)r^4 + A(2c_0^2 - \mathcal{E}^2)r^3 + \left[A^2\left(\frac{7}{4}c_0^2 - \frac{3}{8}\mathcal{E}^2\right) - B^2 c_0^2\right]r^2 + 2B^2 c_0^2 A r - \frac{3}{4}B^2 c_0^2 A^2}}$$

$$= \frac{B}{\sqrt{c_0^2-\mathcal{E}^2}} \cdot \frac{2\pi}{\sqrt{r_1 r_2}}\left[1 + \frac{1}{2}\left(\frac{1}{r_1} + \frac{1}{r_2}\right)\left(-A + \underbrace{-\frac{1}{2}\frac{d}{c}}_{-2A}\right)\right]$$

$$\sqrt{r_1 r_2} = \sqrt{-c} = \sqrt{\frac{c_0^2 B^2}{c_0^2 - \mathcal{E}^2}}$$

Faktor $\frac{1}{2}$ vor dem ganzen Integral vergessen.

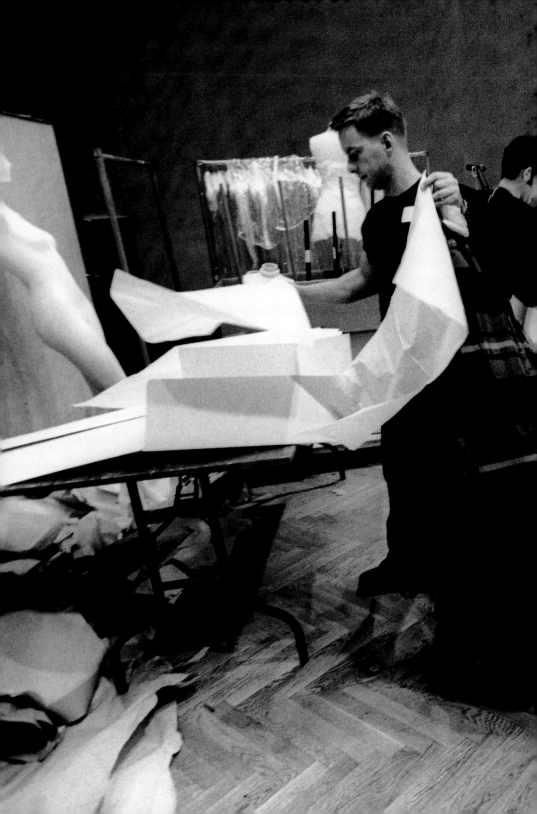

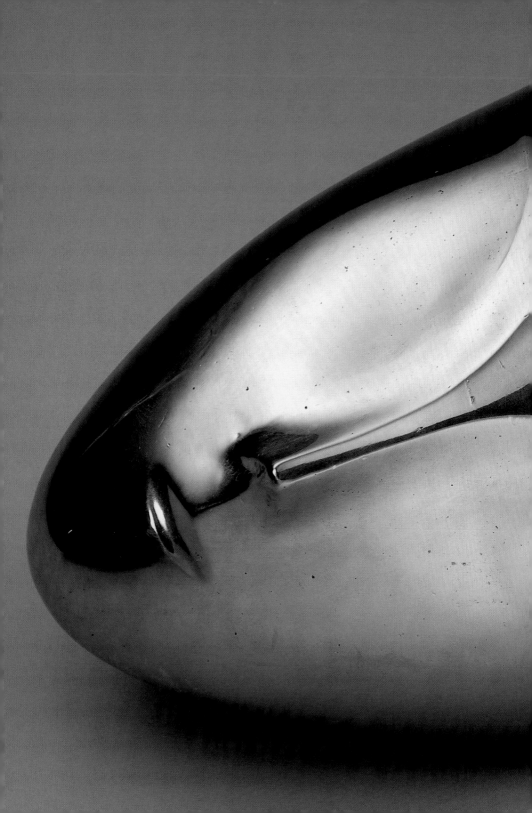

Incipit epistola sancti iheronimi ad
paulinum presbiterum de omnibus
diuine historie libris. capitulū pmū.

Rater ambrosius
tua michi munus-
cula pferens: detulit
sit et suauissimas
lras: q a principio
amicicias: fide pba-
re iam fidei z veteris amicicie noua:
pferebant. Vera eni illa necessitudo e-
z xpi glutino copulata: quin non vtili-
tas rei familiaris: nō pntia tantum
corporr: nō sdbola z palpās adulaco:
sed dei timor: z diuinaq scripturarū
studia conciliant. Legimus in veteri-
bus historijs: quosdā lustrasse puincias
nouos adijsse pplos: maria trāsisse:
ut eos quos ex libris noueranr: corā
qz viderer. Sicut pitagoras memphi-
ticos vates: sic plato egiptū: z archita
tarentinū: eandemq oram ytalie: que
quondā magna grecia dicebaer: labo-
riosissime peragrauit: et ut qui atheniis
mgr erar: z potens: cuiusqz doctrinas
achademie gignasia psonabant: fieret
peginus atqz discipulus: malens aliena
verecude discere: qin sua impudent ingere.
Deniqz cū lras quasi toto orbe fugien-
tes psequit: capt a piratis z venūda-
tus: tyrāno crudelissimo paruit: duct
captiuus vinct z seruus. Tame quia
pfus maior emente se fuit: ad crytum
liuiū: lacteo eloquencie fonte manantē:
de vlcimis hispanie galliarūqz finibus
quosdam venisse nobiles legimus: z
quos ad contemplacione sui roma nō
traxerat: unus hois fama pduxit. Ha-
buit illa etas inauditū ōnibus seculis:
celebrandūqz miraclm: ut urbē tanta

ingressi: aliud extra urbem quererent.
Apolloniuus siue ille mag9 ut uulgus
loquitur: siue pfus: ut pitagorici tra-
dunt: intrauit psas: ptāsiuit caucasū:
albanos: scithas: massagetas: opulē-
tissima indie regna penetrauit: et ad
extremum latissimo physon ampne
trāsmisso puenit ad bragmanas: ut
hyarcam in throno sedentē aureo et de
tantali fonte potantem: inter paucos
discipulos: de natura: de moribz: ac de
cursu dieq et sideq audiret docentem.
Inde p elamitas: babilonios: chalde-
os: medos: assyrios: parthos: syros:
phenices: arabes: palestinos: reuersus
ad allexandriā: perrexit ad ethiopiā:
ut gignosophistas z famosissimam
solis mensam viderer in sabulo. Inue-
nit ille vir ubiqz qz disceret: et semp
proficiēs: semp se melior fieret. Scrip-
sit super hoc plenissime octo volumi-
nibus: phylostratus.

Quid loquar de seculi hominibz:
cū apsus paulus: vas eleccois:
z magister gentiū: qui de consciencia
tāti in se hospitis loquebat dicens. An
experimentū queritis eius qui in me
loquitur xpr. Post damascū arabiāqz
lustrata: ascendit iherosolimā ut videt
petrū z māsit apud eū diebz quindeci.
Hoc eni mistio ebdomadis et ogdo-
adis: futur9 gentiū pdicator instruen-
dus erat. Rursusqz post ānos qtuor-
decim assumpto barnaba et tyto: expo-
suit cū apsis euāgeliū: ne forte in va-
cuum currerer aut cucurisset. Habet
nescio qd latentis energie: viue vocis
actus: et in aures discipli de auctoris
ore trāsfusa: foreius sonat. Vnde et
eschineus cū rodi exularet: z legeretur

Colored Stones.

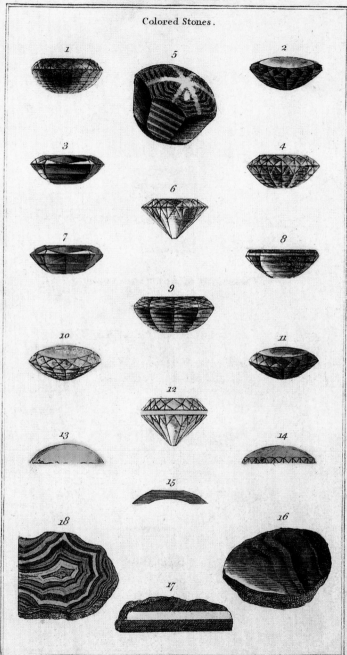

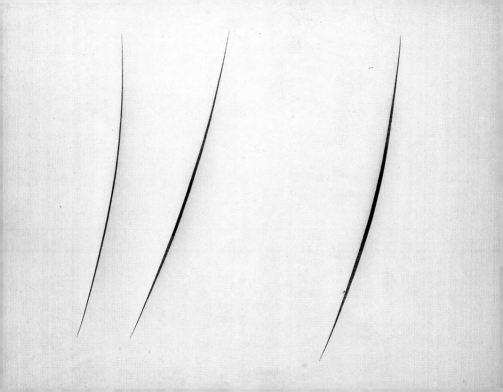

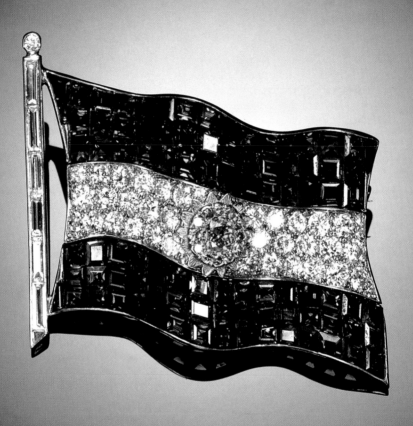

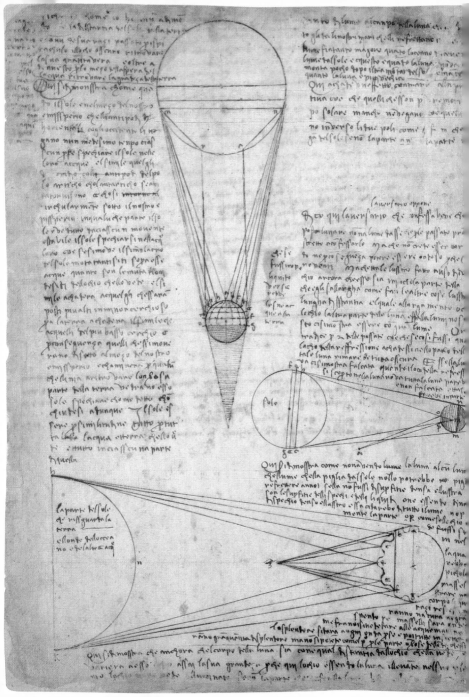

Ogni corpo più denso che lara e men graue dissanaria sere sopra questa faccia et me
causa sostiene. Aduque se lacqua fussi nella luna ella spargiereb... che se alcuna co
uebbe uenire lauostra terra ... di cui ... luna lago capresserebbe... suo pelo...

Qui si rispode esse lacqua nella luna et ...
acqua della terra sopra la quale lacqua si sostiene et coseque a linea elemen esso fis...
se lassa lacqua infralli et ... altri elemen come quagia lauostra no infralli et tam...
sua coseque esse puno velli nostri et la necessario ... lara della luna
più tosto ... se accade se lacqua come corpo più graue dellacqua ... onde no qua
to esse e manifesto sopra se nostre ... menti la quale la su e la terra si sostiene es...
... sua elemen come li elemen graui e leui augu si sospingano in ...
più che leno leu

Qui in questa parte si rispode... dessella...

Del onde dellacq

Londa delmoto dellacq ... e più tarda del ...
luce che lcorso dellacqua che genera lonte delle ... semple dellonte de prati

Londa dellacqua ... ... del siume ... e più tarda del corso dellacqua ...
la genera coquesto acade per lonta ... gusimili siume ... dal sonto dello si
che leco ... si copone moto ... si fugge ... onde
molte son sevole dellonte dellacqua che lento suo siume ... corso e molte
uolte meontrario ... ...
... dellonte ... penetra nelmoto della ... Londa dellacqua ...
... circulare corre dalcerchio ... ... e pone si fecte dellonte alcerchio
lonta di ... triangulare ... no son ... ... p no esse si la
... cerchio dellonte ... dallobietto ... lacqua corrente ... ...

Chronology

1766: 5 December, James Christie holds his first sale in a room in Pall Mall.

1778: James Christie valves Sir Robert Walpole's collection of pictures and negotiates their sale on behalf of his grandson, George Walpole, 3rd Earl of Oxford, to Catherine the Great of Russia.

1795: Sale of Sir Joshua Reynolds's collection.

1803: James Christie's son (also James Christie) takes over business on his father's death.

1831: On the death of James Christie, William Manson joins the firm which becomes Christie & Manson.

1859: Christie, Manson & Woods is formed when Thomas Woods joins the firm.

1919: The last in a series of seven sales of gifts to the Red Cross, held since 1915, brings the aggregate total raised to over £413,405.

1926: Romney's *Portrait of Mrs Davenport* becomes the most expensive work of art sold between the two world wars at £60,900.

1941: Christie's premises suffer a direct hit during the Blitz and moves to Derby House, London.

1953: Christie's moves back into the rebuilt premises at 8 King Street.

1958: Christie's Rome is established.

1968: Christie's open their first base outside the UK in Geneva for international jewellery sales.

1970: Velázquez's portrait of Juan de Pareja fetches £2,310,000, the first work of art to sell at auction for more than £1 million.
Christie's hold their first sale at the Villa Miani in Rome and open a Paris office on rue de Lille.

1973: Christie's becomes a public company quoted on the London Stock Exchange.
Christie's Amsterdam is established.

1975: Christie's South Kensington is established.

1977: Christie's open in New York, with their first series of sales at Park Avenue raising $5 million.

1979: Opening of a second saleroom, Christie's East, in New York.

1985: Mantegna's *Adoration of the Magi* becomes the most expensive Old Master painting ever sold at £8.1 million.
Christie's opens in Monte Carlo and organises its first sale there.

1986: Manet's *La Rue Mosnier aux paveurs* becomes the most expensive Impressionist painting at £7.7 million.
First sale in Hong Kong.
Historic sale of the Nanking Cargo in Amsterdam for £10.2 million.

1987: Van Gogh's *Sunflowers* sells for £24.75 million. Other records include: £7.48 million for a work by Degas, £3.26 million for a Gutenberg Bible, £3.84 million for a 64.83 carat D Flawless diamond and £5.5 million for a Bugatti Royale motor car.

1989: Christie's forms a joint-venture company, Christie's Swire (Hong Kong) Limited and opens a saleroom in Melbourne, Australia.
Christie's Paris moves from rue de Lille to rue Paul Baudry.
Major new development and expansion of King Street premises, doubling salerooms and galleries.

Can dogs bid, too? Spotted at a jewellery sale in Geneva.
© Photo Sasha Gusov/Christie's Images Ltd. 1999.

1990: Offices are opened in Athens, Berlin, Bordeaux, Frankfurt, Gothenburg, Lyon, Singapore and Taiwan.

1991: A sale of Old Master paintings and gold and silverware organised in New York for the Republic of the Philippines raises $20 million with 100 percent sold.

1992: Christie's negotiates the sale of Hans Holbein's *Portrait of a Lady with Squirrel*, belonging to the Marquis of Cholmondeley, to the National Gallery for £10 million. Christie's also arranges the sale of Antonello da Messina's *Cristo alla colonna* [*Christ at the Column*], the property of a private collector, to the Louvre. At £10.1 million, Canaletto's *The Old Horse Guards, London* establishes a record for the artist, the second highest price ever paid for an Old Master and the highest bid for a work of art in two years.

1993: First sales in Athens, Milan, Singapore and Taipei.
Acquisition of the London antique dealer Spinks & Son Ltd., specialising in the trade of coins, Oriental art and British pictures.

1994: First sale in Tel Aviv.
Offices opened in Bombay, Buenos Aires, Lugano, Santiago and Vancouver. Christie's also opens in Shangai to become the first auction company to set up in China.
The contents of Houghton Hall in Britain are auctioned for £21.3 million, a record for a private collection of art and furniture.

1995: Christie's takes over Great Estates, an American real estate company.
First sale in Los Angeles.
Offices opened in Brisbane, Florence and Seoul.
Christie's is the first auction company to hold a sale in China.
Christie's sets up a web site.

1996: Offices opened in Barcelona, Jakarta, Kuala Lumpur and Prague.
Extension of Christie's South Kensington premises with the opening of the Europa Gallery.

1997: Opening of a saleroom in Los Angeles.
June, New York, Christie's sells 69 dresses belonging to Diana, Princess of Wales, for $3.2 million donated to Aids and cancer research.
Hubert de Givenchy appointed President of Christie's France.
Christie's negotiates the sale of David's *Portrait of Juliette de Villeneuve* to the Société des amis du Louvre.
November, New York, Christie's sells the Ganz Collection of Modern and Contemporary Art from $207 million, a record for a single-owner sale at auction.

1998: Office opened in Bangkok, Thailand.
June, acquisition of Christie's by Artémis, the holding company of François Pinault.
July, London, Geoffrey Chaucer's *Canterbury Tales*, printed by William Caxton in 1476–1477 is sold for £4.6 million, a record for a printed book.
November, New York. Van Gogh's *Portrait de l'artiste sans barbe* is sold for $71.5 million.

1999: Opening of new offices and salerooms, Rockefeller Center, New York and in avenue Matignon, Paris.

Lord Hindlip, Chairman of Christie's International, at the rostrum during the auction in June 1997 in New York of dresses belonging to Diana, Princess of Wales. © Photo Ron Frehm-AP/Boomerang.

Christie's

James Christie. A portrait painted by Thomas Gainsborough (1727-1728), his friend and neighbour, in 1778. The J. Paul Getty Museum, Los Angeles. © The J. Paul Getty Museum.
The King of Epithets. A 1782 caricature by H. Humphrey of James Christie, nicknamed "the King of epithets" on account of his saleroom banter. © Christie's Images Ltd. 1999.

A Peep at Christie's. A Rowlandson caricature showing the Earl of Derby with his mistress, the actress Miss Farren who became his second wife. Her nickname of Nimeney Pimeney derived from a role she played in General Burgoyne's play *Heiress.* © Christie's Images Ltd. 1999.
The sale catalogue for the jewels of Madame Du Barry. © Christie's Images Ltd. 1999.

Sino-tibetan lamaist figure ; *The Walking Man I,* Giacometti ; vintage wines ; *Studies of a man's head and hand,* Raphael ; *Codex Leicester,* Vinci ; *Victory* diamond ; 18th century vase ; Louis XV Sávonnerie carpet ; *Liberty* coin ; evening coat dress, Balenciaga ; violincello, Stradivari ; *Shot Red Marilyn,* Warhol ; George III sofa, Adam et Chippendale ; Louis XV tureen, Juste-Aurèle ; mesopotamian casket ; *Blind hurdy-gurdy player,* La Tour ; *Doctor Gachet,* Van Gogh. © Christie's Images Ltd. 1999.

Christie's auction room. A watercolour by Thomas Rowlandson. © Christie's Images Ltd. 1999.

Hanging paintings at Christie's New York for the preview of "Arts of France", an annual sale of 18th century French art. © Photo Sasha Gusov/Christie's Images Ltd. 1999.

Duke Cosimo I de Medici, Pontormo. Portrait sold for $35.2 million (£22.3 million) in 1989 in New York: a new record for an Old Master. © Christie's Images Ltd. 1999.
Le Rêve, Picasso, 1932. Painting from the Victor and Sally Ganz collection – the biggest single-owner sale ever –, sold for $48.2 million in New York, 10 November 1997. © Succession Picasso/Christie's Images Ltd. 1999.

Sunflowers, **Van Gogh.** Sold in London for £24.75 million in March 1987. © Christie's Images Ltd. 1999.

Lord Huidlip Charles Allsopp during the Van Gogh's *Sunflowers* auction. © Christie's Images Ltd. 1999.

Muhammad Ali. The Paloger collection of memorabilia was sold in Beverly Hills, California, in October 1997 for $1,321,905.

Untitled, **Jean-Michel Basquiat,** coloured oilsticks on paper, sold in New York on 8 October 1992 for $4,000. © Christie's Images Ltd. 1999.

Benin bronze head prior to 1550, sold in July 1989 in London for £1,320,000. © Christie's Images Ltd. 1999.

Cuneiform clay tablets (ancient Middle Eastern) from the Erlenmeyer collection. © Christie's Images Ltd. 1999.

Albert Einstein in Pasadena, California, in 1931. © Photo Upi/Corbis-Bettmann/Sipa Press.

Einstein's manuscript on the theory of relativity sold for $398,500 at Christie's New York in 1996. © Christie's Images Ltd. 1999.

The sales of the Rudolf Nureyev collection in London and New York totalled £6.8 million ($10 million). The dancer's ballet slippers sold for £12,000. © Christie's Images Ltd. 1999.

Nureyev in the bathroom of his apartment on quai Voltaire on Paris's Left Bank. © Rue des Archives/Everett.

Christie's sale of dresses belonging to Diana, Princess of Wales, provoked enormous media interest (June 1997). © Photo Sasha Gusov/Christie's Images Ltd. 1999.

La Muse endormie II, **Brancusi.** Polished bronze, cast in the mid 1920's and sold in New York in November 1997 for $6,602,500. © Christie's Images Ltd. 1999.

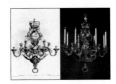

Chandelier for the King, a drawing by the architect William Kent, from John Vardy's *Some designs of Mr. Inigo Jones and Mr. William Kent,* London 1744, plate 23.
The silver Hanover Chandelier (1736-1737) by Balthasar-Friedrich Behrens, from a drawing by William Kent. © Christie's Images Ltd. 1999.

Gutenberg Bible. The first edition of 1455, sold for $5,390,000 (£3,266,666) in New York in 1987. © Christie's Images Ltd. 1999.
Juan de Pareja, **Velázquez.** Portrait of a slave whom the artist freed and a painter in his own right. The painting fetched £2,310,000 in London in 1970 – a record for an Old Master. © Christie's Images Ltd. 1999.

Central Park, **Childe Hassam,** oil on canvas. Sold for $4,1 million (£2,4 million) on 2 December 1998 in New York. © Christie's Images Ltd. 1999.

Teddy Bear. Sold for a record £110,000 in London on 5 December 1994, this teddy bear had belonged to Colonel "Bob" Henderson, the greatest teddy bear collector in the world. © Christie's Images Ltd. 1999.
Fillette au tablier noir, **Amedeo Modigliani,** 1918. Sold on 30 March 1991 in London for £2,400,000. © Christie's Images Ltd. 1999.

A Treatise on Diamonds by John Mawe (London, 1823). Frontispiece.
Nicholas Brown Bookcase. The magnificent Chippendale mahogany block-and-shell desk and bookcase was sold on 3 June 1989 in New York for $11 million (£6,5 million). © Christie's Images Ltd. 1999

Rest on the Flight into Egypt, **Michelangelo.** Bought by the Getty in July 1993 for £4,181,500, a record price for an Old Master drawing. © Christie's Images Ltd. 1999.

Portrait de l'artiste, Paul Cézanne. Sold on 30 November 1992 in London for £950,000. © Christie's Images Ltd. 1999.
Concetto Spaziale, Attese, Lucio Fontana, 1961-1962. Sold in London, 19 March 1996, for £44,000: © Christie's Images Ltd. 1999.

A Steinway piano decorated by Sir Lawrence Alma-Tadema sold, with a matching pair of stools for £716,500 in London, November 1997. © Photo Sasha Gusov/Christie's Images Ltd. 1999.

An Argentine flag brooch by Van Cleef & Arpels which was sold in New York for $992,500 on 6 April 1998. Formerly the property of Eva Perón. © Christie's Images Ltd.1999.
Eva Perón in August 1949 wearing the same Van Cleef & Arpels brooch. © Archivo General de la Nacion, Argentina.

Contrasts of form, Fernand Léger. Sold on 27 November 1989 in London for £8,500,000. © Christie's Images Ltd. 1999.
Lewis Carroll's photograph of Alice Liddell, the inspiration for *Alice in Wonderland* and *Alice through the Looking-glass,* dressed as a beggar. Albumen print, c. 1858, sold on 9 December 1998 in New York for $55,000. © Christie's Images Ltd. 1999.

A sale of important Indian jewellery, October 1997. Left: a 17th century carved emerald and diamond brooch, sold in London for £150,000. © Christie's Images Ltd. 1999. Right: miniature of a *Mughal lady.* Courtesy of the Victoria & Albert Museum, London. © V&A Picture Library.

Codex Hammer, Leonardo da Vinci, pp. 44-47. Microsoft boss Bill Gates acquired Leonardo da Vinci's manuscript in 1994 for $30.8 million. © Christie's Images Ltd. 1999.

Marilyn and Queen Elizabeth at the Royal Film Premiere for *The Battle of the River Plate* on 29 October 1956. The dress worn by the actress was sold in London on 27 April 1989 for £3,080. © Christie's Images Ltd. 1999/All rights reserved.
A used one penny stamp (New Zealand, 1855), sold in London in February 1989 for £4,675. © Christie's Images Ltd. 1999.

The author would like to thank Marc Alcover, Karin Breuninger, Victoria Coode, Katharina Feller-Baignères, Céline Hersant, Consuelo Moorsom, Jeremy Rex-Parkes, Emma Strouts and Bertrand du Vignaud for the help they have given him. The publishers wish to thank Christie's, and in particular Suzy Korb, François Curiel and Hugues Joffre. Thanks also to the Associated Press, Nicole Chamson (Adagp, Paris), The J. Paul Getty Museum (Los Angeles), Sasha Gusov, the Picasso Administration, Rue des Archives, Sipa Press and the Victoria & Albert Museum (London) for their contribution to this work.